The Little Book of Big Ribbon Ideas

If you haven't discovered the fun of making bows and creating beautiful things with ribbon, you'll be pleasantly surprised at how very easy it is to add ribbon-crafting to your life. It takes very little time to learn and to do. The bows you make can be as simple as a two-loop shoestring tie or as elegant as a multi-layered gift bow — but YOU CAN MAKE THEM ALL — we promise! Leaf through the pages of The Little Book of Big Ribbon Ideas, then choose your favorite spools of ribbon to begin creating scrapbook embellishments, bridal bows, Christmas decorations, gift toppers, and so much more!

Since wee folks spend many hours tying our hearts 'round their little fingers, it's only fitting that their scrapbook pages should be embellished with little bows. Choose navy satin ribbon for a boy, or dainty gingham ribbon for a girl.

Attention-getting bows are just-right additions to special greetings and important news. *Left to right:* Top a handmade valentine with a bow in pink checks. Frame a very special photo by threading a striped grosgrain ribbon through holes punched in card stock. And share your thoughts in a little note that's topped with a pocketful of faux rose petals and closed with a pretty floral bow.

once upon a time...

For instant decoration that offers color, texture, and dimension, ribbon is your best value! Use lengths of ribbon to dangle delicate charms on handcrafted notes. Or try "sewing" a soft border of satin ribbon around a rectangle of decorated cardstock. Spend just a few minutes with ribbon and paper, and you'll be amazed at the beauty your imagination creates!

A decorator classic: Stack pretty boxes, tie with a wire-edge bow, and glue on a large faux flower.

Make just one box extra-special by covering its lid in a mat of woven ribbons! Just pin the ribbons to interfacing and weave them as you go. Wrap the ribbon mat around the box lid and secure with craft glue, then glue on artificial flowers as you please.

Stronger than its beauty would lead you to believe, wide satin ribbon with a wire edge makes an excellent curtain tieback. Just use it to gather your curtain, tie it into a bow, then glue seashells to the knot.

Use sheer and satin wire-edged ribbon to create a romantic magnolia wreath. Make it fresh with real leaves and roses on a florist's wreath form, or make it last by using artificial flowers and greenery.

Ribbon gives instant unity to a display of decorative saucers that cradle precious photos at their centers. To hang your own saucers, begin by layering two wide, wire-edged fabric ribbons. Fold under 2" of one end. On back of ribbons, sew through all layers to add a curtain tieback ring 1" below fold. On front, hide your stitches by sewing a bow and a button to ribbons. Trim free ends of ribbons as you please. Attach spring-grip plate hangers around ribbons and saucers. When ready to display, hang the plate hangers first, then secure the tieback ring.

With ribbon, you've got your decorating all wrapped up! Glue lengths of ribbon to a lampshade and weave a pretty lattice on a memo board for a special touch that everyone will notice.

Sweet ribbons perform a beautiful function on a heart-shaped pillow for a ring bearer.

Instant centerpiece — faux roses, tulle, and a sheer ribbon bow on a grouping of glass vases.

I do, I do! Champagne flutes are surrounded by love, and lovingly embellished with rosebuds and ribbons.

Sculptural beauty on the top of a special cake — roses & ribbons are the perfect pairing.

Breathtaking mini wreaths are amazingly simple to create! For this bridal decoration, start by wiring a pew clip to the back of a floral candle ring. Make a bow of wire-edged ribbon, then attach the bow to the candle ring and pew clip with a second wire-edged bow.

The airy beauty of lace drapes the back of a fold-out chair for a memorable occasion. A half-yard of lace fabric is wired together and tied with a bow of satin-edged ribbon. A stem of bow-tied silk flowers, tucked into the knot of the larger bow, adds an easy touch of elegance.

Sweet simplicity! On the handles of the cake knife and server, tie a small piece of tulle. Top with bows of wire-edged satin ribbon and sheer ribbon before gluing a flower in the center of it all.

Your guests will favor these treats! The tiny "treasure chests" show your wedding colors with artificial flowers and narrow satin ribbon. And everyone will enjoy these bottles of bubbly — soap bubble bottles are wrapped in tulle and finished with flowers and bows.

"Pocket" ribbon makes instant wedding favors. Just cut the ribbon near the pre-stitched lines and fill the pockets with treats. Close with the wire stem of a silk flower; tie with ribbon. For a cherished keepsake, top a photo album with a doily and ribbon roses (pages 31 - 32).

Without a doubt, bows are the best way to add holiday color and creativity to boxes and baskets. These festive ribbons lend cheer to Valentine's Day and Halloween.

A bright bow on an Easter basket will make little chicks chirp happily! And when she sees the pretty bows on her gifts, Mom will know whom you love best on Mother's Day.

Rediscover the richness of a traditional Christmas, at a price even Scrooge would love! Ribbons are inexpensive, yet give you lots of color and cheer with every bow you fashion. Heighten the anticipation by sealing your gifts with a variety of bows, whether simple or sumptuous. And don't forget to tie a little merriment onto your pillows.

Just add a bow to make every ornament on your tree extra-special! Use sheer ribbon to close a gift bag, or add a center loop bow to a pot of poinsettias. For a box that hints of the riches inside, top it with layers of fluffy bows and nestle an ornament among the loops.

General Supplies

Ribbon
24-gauge wire
Wire cutters
Scissors
Lead pencil or white quilting pencil
Miscellaneous supplies

Measuring Ribbon Accurately

"Measure and Mark" method. This method can be used for most bows. The first measurement in each bow instruction is for the streamer; the second measurement is for the loop length. Use a ruler and lightly mark the measurements on the ribbon with a lead pencil (for light color ribbon) or white quilting pencil (for dark color ribbon) before you begin to tie the bow.

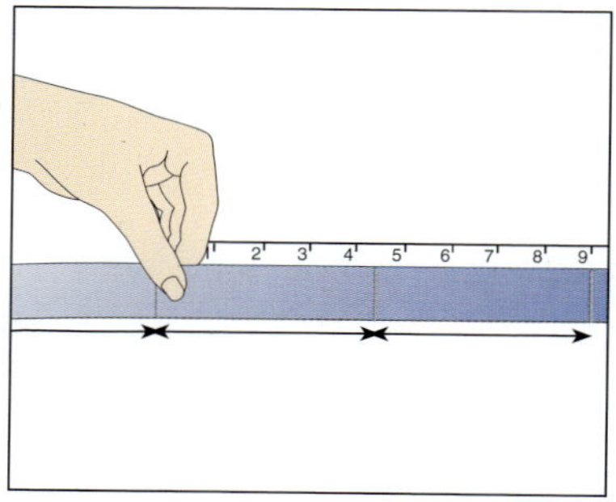

"Measure as You Tie" method. Use this method for ribbons that cannot be marked or if you do not wish to mark on your ribbon. Use a ruler to measure the correct length as you form each loop or streamer.

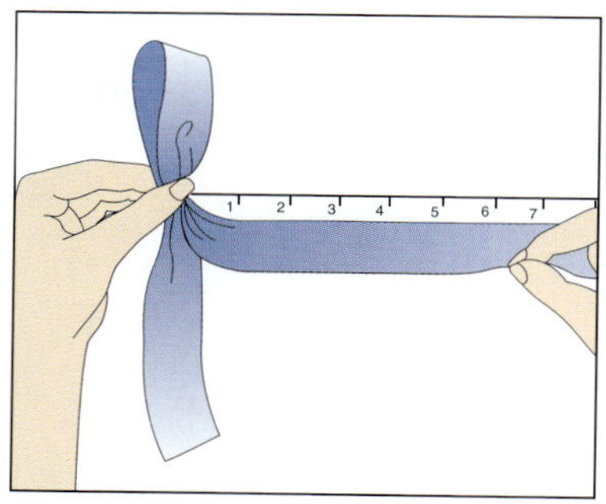

Securing The Bow

1. Place a length of wire across center of bow. Bring wire ends to back of bow.

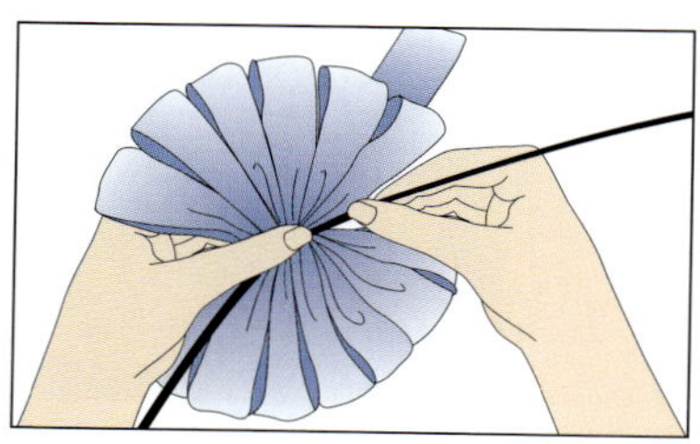

2. Pull loops and streamers forward, away from wire ends. Place index finger between wire ends and against center back of bow; hold wire ends in palm of hand.

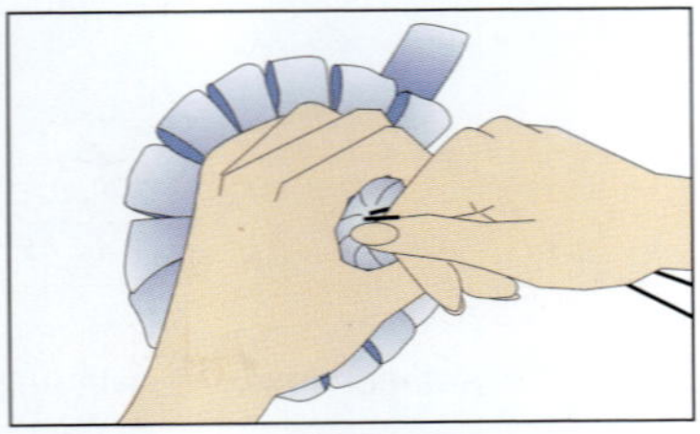

3. Twist bow to tighten wire around center of bow.

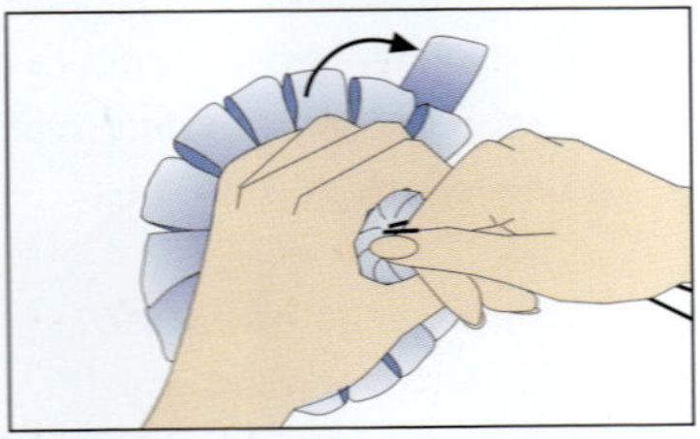

Trimming Streamers

Streamers may be trimmed in a variety of ways including angled, straight across, pointed, or notched. To notch or point a streamer end, fold the streamer in half lengthwise and cut at an angle from the folded edge to the open edge.

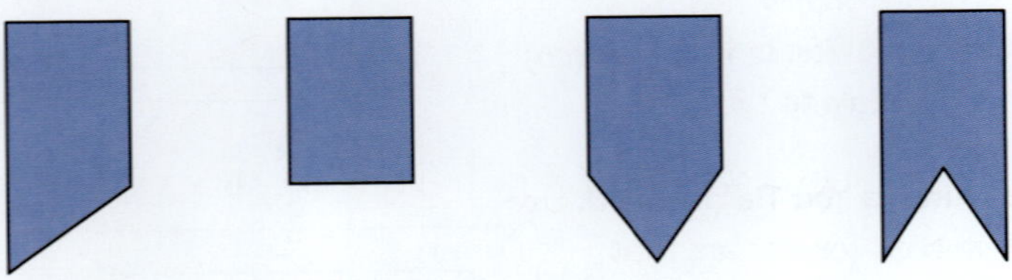

How Much Ribbon Do You Need?

To determine the amount of ribbon you will need for any size bow, follow this guide:

Diameter, in inches, you want the finished bow to be:	______"
Multiply diameter by the number of loops you want:	x ______
Add the length, in inches, of streamers (if any):	+ ______"
Add an additional 6"-12" for gathering and trimming:	+ ______"
Divide by 36 to get the total ribbon yardage needed:	______yds

Floral Bow

For an 8" diameter bow, you will need 2¾ yds of 2⅞" wire-edge ribbon.

1. For first streamer, measure and lightly mark 10" from one end of ribbon. For loops, begin at streamer mark and measure and lightly mark 9" eight times along length of ribbon.

2. Hold ribbon at streamer mark, gathering between thumb and forefinger. Twist remaining ribbon one full turn.

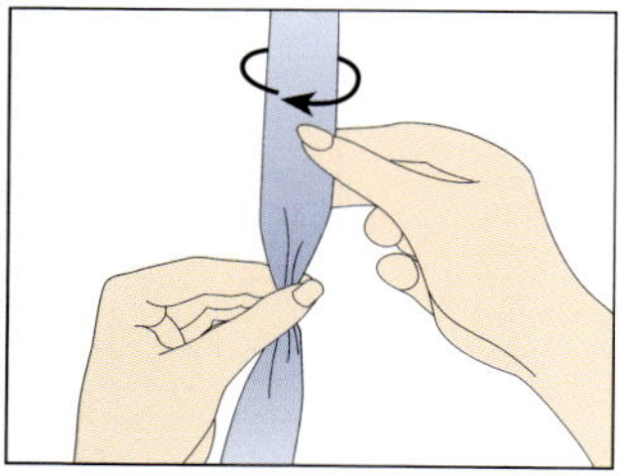

3. To form first loop, place first loop mark behind streamer mark; gather ribbon between thumb and forefinger. Twist remaining ribbon one full turn.

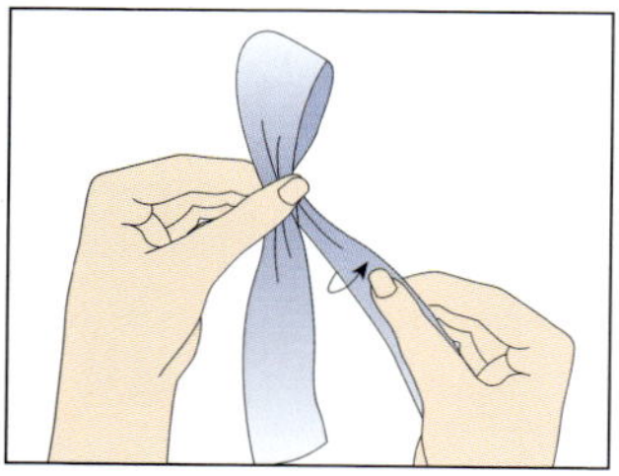

4. To form second loop, place second loop mark behind first loop mark; gather ribbon between thumb and forefinger. Twist remaining ribbon one full turn.

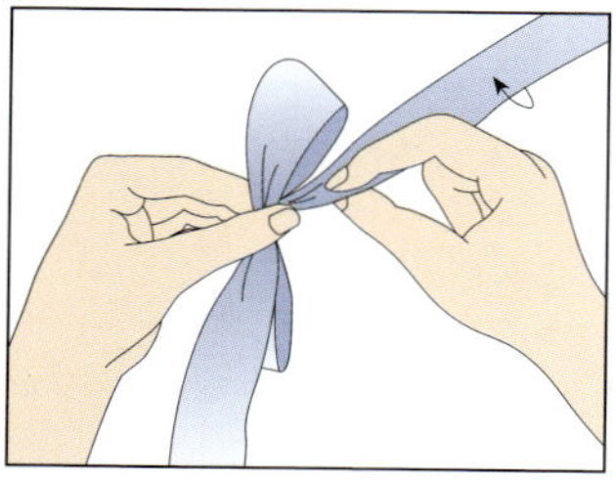

5. Continue placing loop marks behind previous loop marks and twisting remaining ribbon. Complete eight loops.

6. Use wire to secure bow. For second streamer, trim ribbon to 10". Trim streamers and arrange loops.

For a 6" diameter bow, you will need 3¼ yds of 1½" wire-edge ribbon. Follow Steps 1-6, making 10" streamers and twelve 7" loops.

For a 7" diameter bow, you will need 3 yds of 1½" wire-edge ribbon. Follow Steps 1-6, making 10" streamers and ten 8" loops.

Stacked Tie Bow

For a 9" diameter yellow bow with flower center, you will need 1¾ yds of wire-edge ribbon, a silk flower, and a glue gun.

1. For first streamer, measure and lightly mark 10" from one end of ribbon. For loops, begin at streamer mark and measure and lightly mark 8" two times, then 10" two times along length of ribbon.

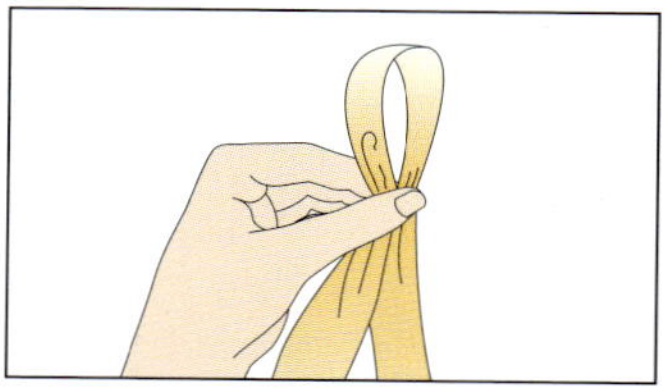

2. To form first loop, place streamer mark next to first loop mark; gather ribbon between thumb and forefinger.

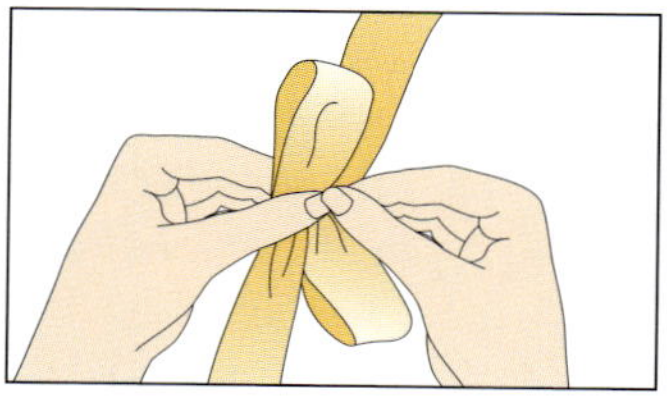

3. To form second loop, place second mark next to gathered center; gather ribbon between thumbs and forefingers.

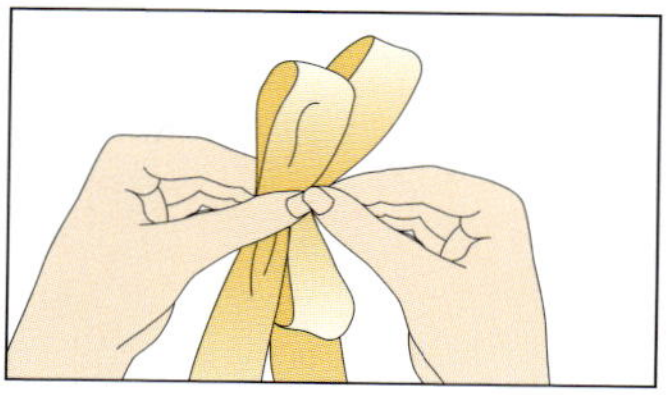

4. While holding first and second loops, place third loop mark behind gathered center, "layering" third loop behind first loop. Gather ribbon between thumbs and forefingers.

5. To form fourth loop, repeat Step 3, "layering" fourth loop behind second loop.

6. Use wire to secure bow. For second streamer, trim ribbon to 10". Trim streamers. Glue silk flower to center of bow.

Shoestring Tie Bow

For a 9" diameter bow, you will need $1\frac{1}{2}$ yds of wire-edge ribbon.

1. For first streamer, measure and lightly mark 10" from one end of ribbon. For first loop, begin at streamer mark and measure and lightly mark 10".

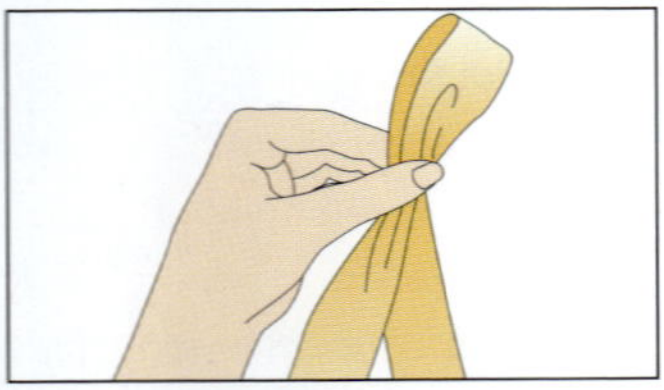

2. To form first loop, place first loop mark behind streamer mark; gather ribbon between thumb and forefinger.

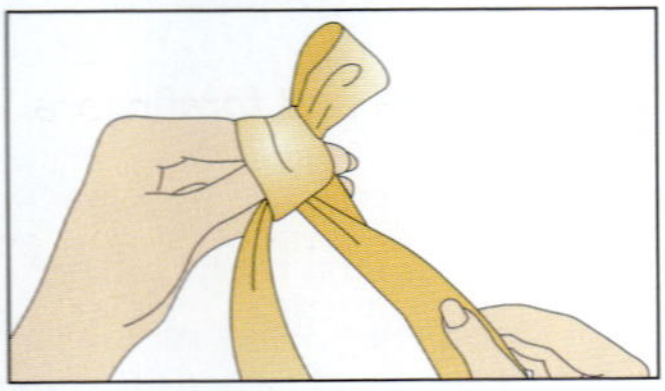

3. Loosely wrap remaining length of ribbon once around thumb. To form second loop, fold remaining ribbon approximately 4" from wrapped area; slide folded end of ribbon through wrapped area.

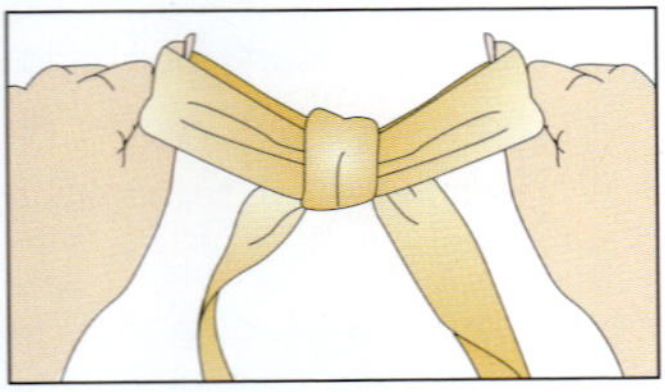

4. Place thumbs inside loops. Pull the loops to tighten bow. Adjust size of loops by pulling on streamers.

For a $7\frac{1}{2}$" diameter multi-ribbon bow, you will need $1\frac{1}{4}$ yds each of five different ribbons. Hold all ribbons together and follow Steps 1-4, measuring 7" for first loop.

Center Loop Bow

For a 9" diameter bow, you will need $2^1/_2$ yds of $2^7/_8$" wire-edge ribbon.

1. For first streamer, measure and lightly mark 10" from one end of ribbon. For center loop, begin at streamer mark and measure and lightly mark 6". For loops, begin at center loop mark and measure and lightly mark 9" six times along length of ribbon.

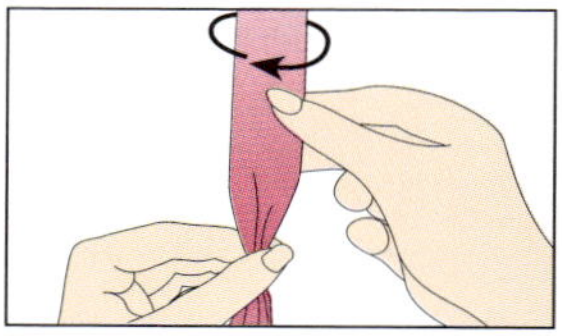

2. Hold ribbon at streamer mark, gathering between thumb and forefinger. Twist remaining ribbon one full turn.

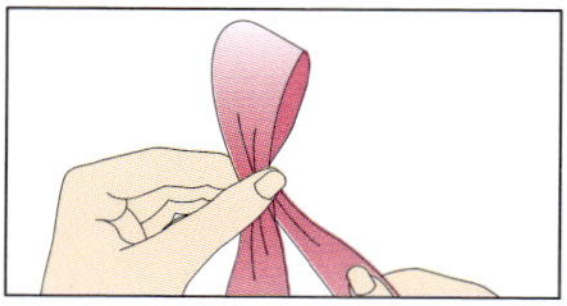

3. To form center loop, place center loop mark behind streamer mark; gather ribbon between thumb and forefinger.

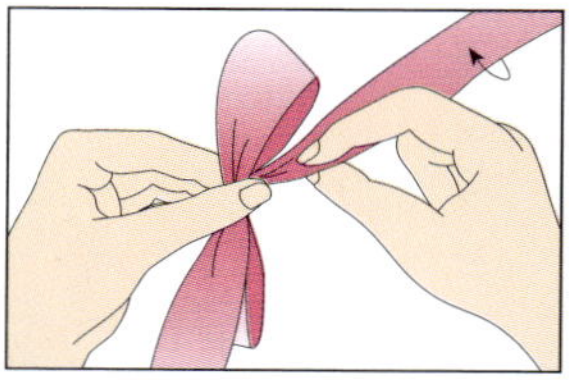

4. To form first loop, place first loop mark behind center loop mark; gather ribbon between thumb and forefinger. Twist remaining ribbon one full turn.

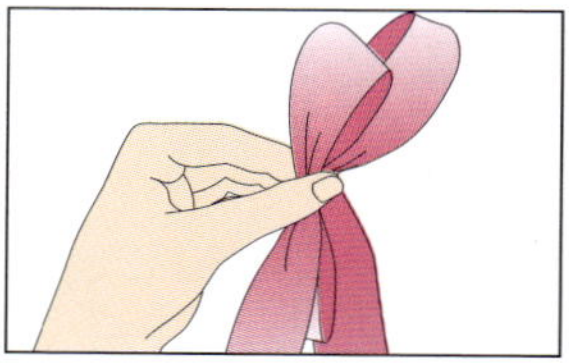

5. To form second loop, place second loop mark behind first loop mark; gather ribbon between thumb and forefinger. Twist remaining ribbon one full turn.

6. Continue placing loop marks behind previous loop marks and twisting remaining ribbon. Complete six loops.

7. Use wire to secure bow. For second streamer, trim ribbon to 10". Trim streamers and arrange loops.

Creative Combinations

For an 8" diameter bow with a contrasting center, you will need 4½ yds of 2⅞" wire-edge ribbon and 1¼ yds of 1½" ribbon. Use the 2⅞" ribbon and follow **Easiest Bow Ever** (page 28), wrapping ribbon eight times. Use the 1½" ribbon and follow **Shoestring Tie Bow** (page 25), measuring 6" for first loop. Wire the small bow to center of large bow.

For a 4" diameter bow with a cord center, you will need ¾ yd of 1½" ribbon and ¾ yd of cord. Use the 1½" ribbon and follow **Easiest Bow Ever** (page 28), wrapping only two times **widthwise**. Cut a 17" length and a 7" length from cord; tie a knot in each end of both cords. Holding both cords together, tie around center of bow; tie a small **Shoestring Tie Bow** (page 25) using longer cord.

Easiest Bow Ever

For this bow, you will need $2\frac{1}{2}$ yds of $1\frac{1}{2}$" wire-edge ribbon.

1. Wrap ribbon around Little Book **lengthwise** five times.

2. Use wire to secure **each side** of ribbon.

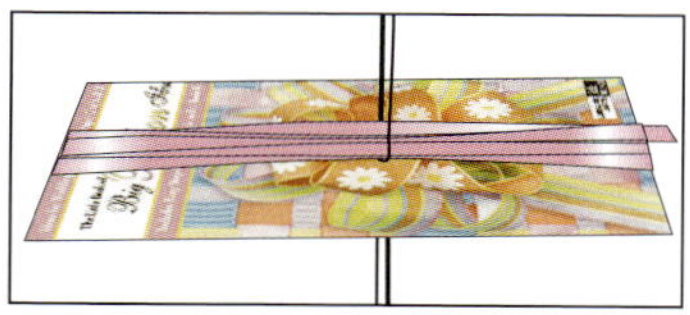

3. Slide ribbon off Little Book. Pinch ribbons together where wires meet; use wires to secure bow.

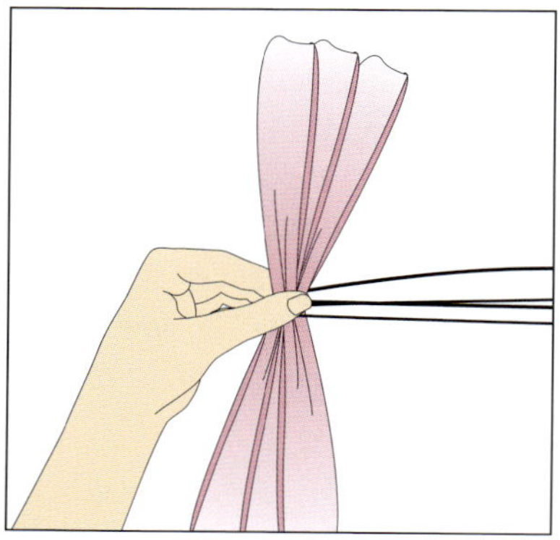

4. Cut streamers and arrange loops.

For this bow, you will need 1½ yds of 7/8" wire-edge ribbon. Follow **Easiest Bow Ever**, wrapping ribbon **widthwise** around Little Book.

For a bow with flower center, you will need 1¼ yds of 7/8" ribbon, a silk flower, and a glue gun. Follow **Easiest Bow Ever**, wrapping ribbon four times **widthwise** around Little Book. Glue flower to center of bow.

For this sheer ribbon bow, you will need 2 yds of 7/8" ribbon. Follow **Easiest Bow Ever**, wrapping ribbon four times **widthwise** around Little Book.

For the wide sheer ribbon bow, you will need a 3 yd spool of $2^7/_8$" wire-edge ribbon. Follow **Easiest Bow Ever** (page 28), wrapping ribbon around Little Book until ribbon is used up.

For the bow with small bow center, you will need $1^1/_2$ yds of $1^1/_2$" wired ribbon and $1^1/_4$ yds of $^7/_8$" ribbon. Using $1^1/_2$" ribbon, follow **Easiest Bow Ever** (page 28), wrapping ribbon **lengthwise** around Little Book three times. Repeat using $^7/_8$" ribbon, wrapping ribbon four times **widthwise** around Little Book. Wire small bow to center of large bow.

Ribbon Roses

For large ribbon rose, you will need $18^1/_2$" of $1^1/_2$" wire-edged ribbon and floral tape.

For medium ribbon rose, you will need 12" of $^7/_8$" wire-edged ribbon and floral tape.

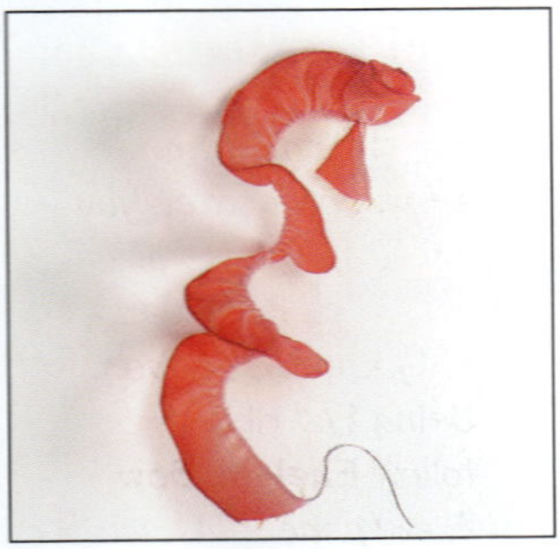

1. To make each rose, make a knot at one end of the ribbon length. At opposite end, pull wire from one side and gently slide ribbon along wire until entire side is completely gathered; do not cut off wire end.
2. To form rose, begin with knotted end and spiral wrap gathered ribbon around knot. Wrap tightly at first, to form center of rose, then loosely for open petals.
3. To end, fold raw edge under rose and wrap wire tightly around knotted end; trim excess wire. Wrap base of rose with floral tape.

For ribbon rosebud, you will need 7" of $1^1/_2$" wire-edged ribbon, sewing thread and needle, and floral tape.

1. To make rosebud, hold ribbon horizontally and fold one end down $1^1/_2$" at a 90-degree angle for stem (**A**).
2. To form center of bud, roll edge of ribbon toward unfolded end two times. With one hand holding base of bud center and other hand holding unfolded or working end of ribbon, fold working ribbon up at a 90-degree angle (**B**). At the same time, turn the center a turn or two toward the working end. Continue folding the working end and turning the center until ribbon length is used up.
3. Fold working end of ribbon down and twist it together with stem. Using needle, wrap thread tightly around stem, taking a few stitches to secure. Wrap end with floral tape.

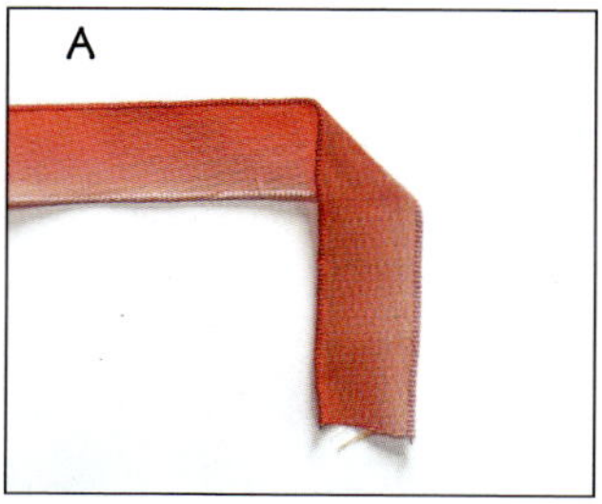

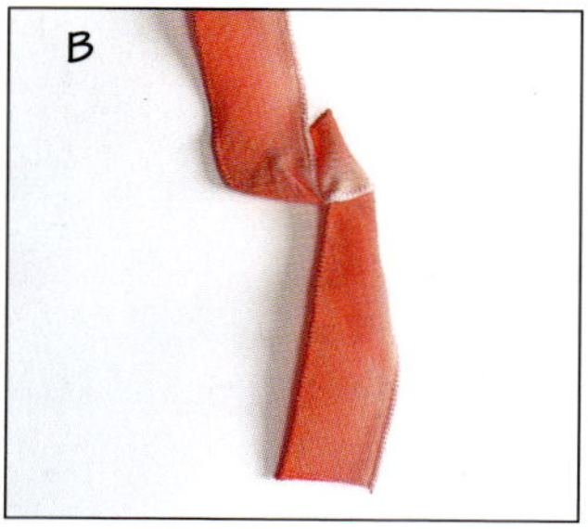

For leaf, you will need 7"of $^7/_8$" wire-edged ribbon, floral tape, and fabric glue.

1. Fold ribbon length in half, matching long edges. Slide both ends of ribbon along wire on one edge, forming tight gathers for leaf center. Twist wire ends together to secure; trim excess wire.
2. Fold raw edges in and wrap base of leaf with floral tape. Use fingers to shape leaf. Apple a thin line of fabric glue along back of leaf center to hold ribbon edges together.